First published in The United States by **Holland Brown Books, LLC** 2010
The Green Building
732 East Market Street
Louisville, Kentucky 40202
USA

www.hollandbrownbooks.com

Copyright © 2010 Holland Brown Books
Manufactured by Friesens Corporation in Altona, MB, Canada (August, 2010)
D#58157

ISBN 13: 978-0-9797006-3-7
ISBN 10: 0-9797006-3-9
Library of Congress Control Number: 2010932496

Baltimore Counts! A Children's Counting Book
1st Edition

By Siri Lise Doub and Wayne Arnold
Edited by J. Gill Holland and Stephanie Brothers

Contributing Artists
Carbery Morrow, Marion Stern, Tom Chalkley, Bonnie Matthews, Jessica Pegorsch, Amanda Brodsky,
Wayne Arnold, Kevin O'Malley, Taylor Goff, Cristian A. Alba, Michel Modell, Annie Gray Robrecht,
Anne Stiebing, Jennifer Berk, Mary Gearhart, Maren Hassinger, Ava Hassinger, Kim Manfredi,
Melody Often, Steve Baker, Mina Cheon, Kenny Yee, Siiri Poldmae, Gregg Simonton,
Michelle La Perriere, Jeffrey Kent, and Melissa Dickenson

Creative input by Astri and Poe Doub
Cover Illustrations by James R. Long

The moral rights of the authors and artists have been reserved.

Typeset and Printed in Canada.

For Robb, Astri and Poe

BALTIMORE COUNTS!

A Children's Counting and Art Book

by **Siri Lise Doub** and **Wayne Arnold**

Perryville Counts!
W. Arnold

edited by **J. Gill Holland** and **Stephanie Brothers**

With generous contributions from these **Baltimore artists:**

Carbery Morrow, Marion Stern, Tom Chalkley, Bonnie Matthews,

Jessica Pegorsch, Amanda Brodsky, Wayne Arnold, Kevin O'Malley, Taylor Goff,

Cristian A. Alba, Michel Modell, Annie Gray Robrecht, Anne Stiebing,

Jennifer Berk, Mary Gearhart, Maren Hassinger, Ava Hassinger, Kim Manfredi,

Melody Often, Steve Baker, Mina Cheon, Kenny Yee, Siiri Poldmae,

Gregg Simonton, Michelle La Perriere, Jeffrey Kent, Melissa Dickenson

Thanks and gratitude to Gill Holland and everyone who played a part in the creation of Baltimore Counts!

All profits from the sale of this book, as well as half of the sale of corresponding artworks, go directly to OrchKids, an after-school music program in Baltimore city.

O games missed by Oriole Cal Ripken, Jr., in 17 seasons.

1 Baltimore has One Shot Tower. It was once the tallest building in the United States.

M.Stern

2 dinosaur teeth were found outside **Baltimore** in 1858. A local dentist sliced them for a study and saw stars.

ASTRODON AND ACROCANTHOSAURUS
RECONSTRUCTIONS by HALL TRAIN
at the MARYLAND SCIENCE CENTER,
• BALTIMORE •

"STAR TOOTH"

CROSS-SECTION

A Baltimore Checkerspot butterfly has **3** colors: Its body is dark brown.

Its wings are spotted white.
The wing tips are orange.

July **4**, 1828, was the birthday of the Baltimore-Ohio Railroad, the first U.S. **railroad** to carry people.

INTERESTING FACTS ABOUT THE BALTIMORE OHIO RAILROAD COMPANY

1. TWO FRIENDS STARTED WITH A DREAM

2. THEY DID RESEARCH AND TRAVELED TO ENGLAND.

3. THEY MET REALLY IMPORTANT PEOPLE

4. WITH MONEY AND SUPPORT THEY STARTED PREPARING FOR THE RAILROAD.

5. ON JULY 4, 1828 THEY BEGAN CONSTRUCTION

There are **5** letters in Marin & Alsop. Marin Alsop is the director of the Baltimore Symphony Orchestra. She is the first woman to lead an American orchestra.

6

Built in 1693, Fort Garrison is the oldest building in Baltimore County. A captain and 6 rangers guarded trade routes from lookouts on top.

Maryland is the **7**th state of the union. We joined in 1788.

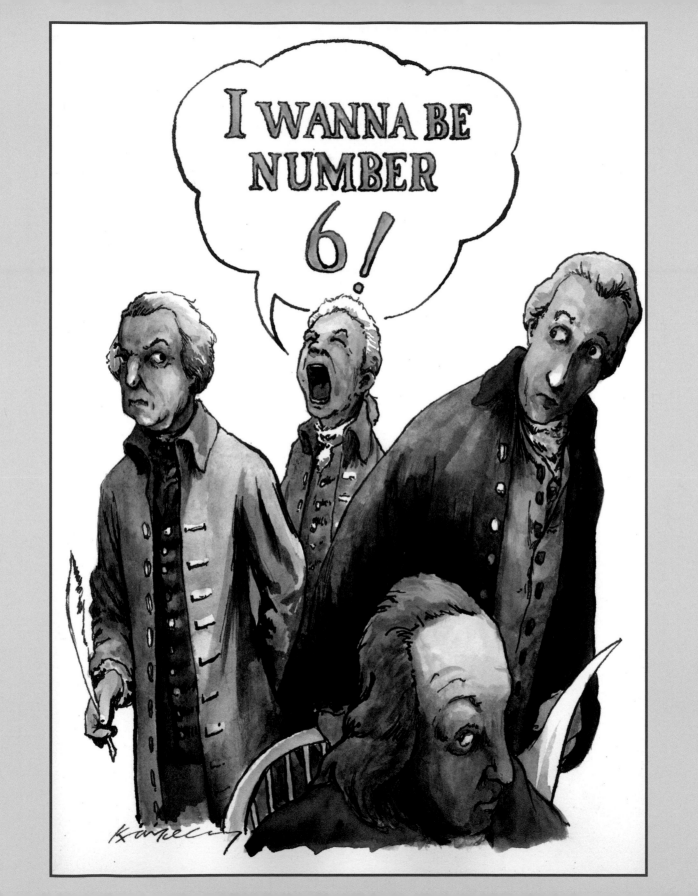

Maryland's black and white Holsteins can produce **8** gallons of milk per day. Milk is our state drink.

There are justices on the **9** U.S. Supreme Court. Thurgood Marshall was the first African-American justice.

Baltimore is the home of the first umbrella factory in the United States. The frame was made of whale bone and weighed

10 pounds.

Baltimore has sister cities throughout the **11** **world: Rotterdam, Netherlands; Luxor, Egypt; Ashkelon, Israel; Bremerhaven, Germany; Genoa, Italy; Xiamen, China; Piraeus, Greece; Odessa, Ukraine; Gbarnga, Liberia; and Kawasaki, Japan.**

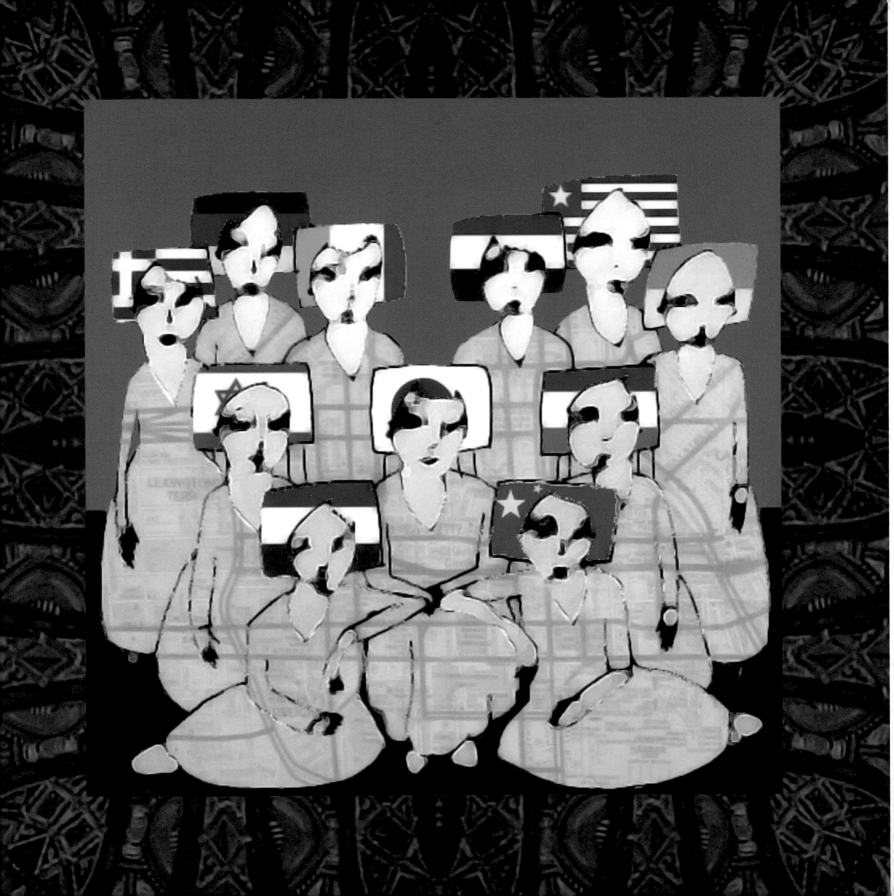

12 letters in "thoroughbred."
These mighty horses stand about 16 hands high. They weigh more than 1,000 pounds and can run up to 40 miles an hour.

13 year-old Edward Warren was the first American to fly. In 1784 he went up in a hot-air balloon.

On September 1814, Francis Scott Key **14,** wrote the Star Spangled Banner as he watched the British Navy attack Fort McHenry.

Lacrosse is the oldest sport in North America.

Native Americans played with up to 1,000 players on fields as long as 15 miles.

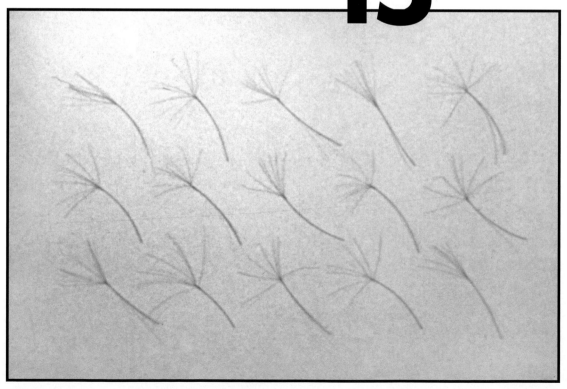

Michael Phelps won a record total of **16** medals in his first two Olympic Games.

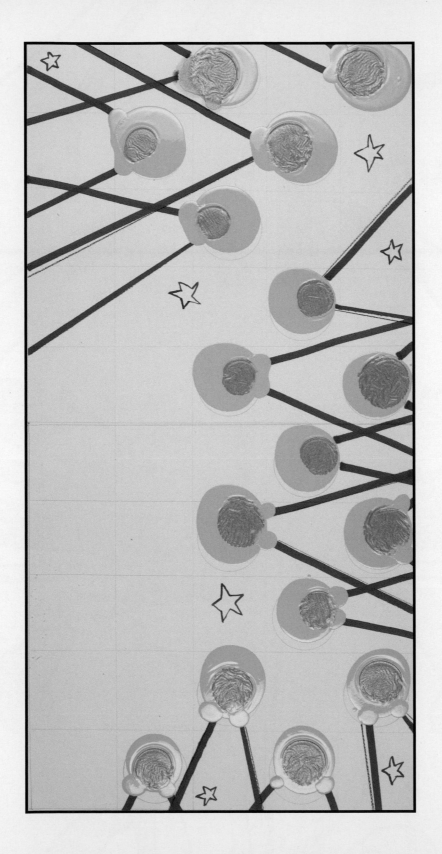

Count **17** crabs.

More than 1/3 of the nation's blue crabs come from the Chesapeake Bay.
YUMMY!

The Chesapeake Bay holds more than **18** trillion gallons of water. It is the largest estuary in the United States.

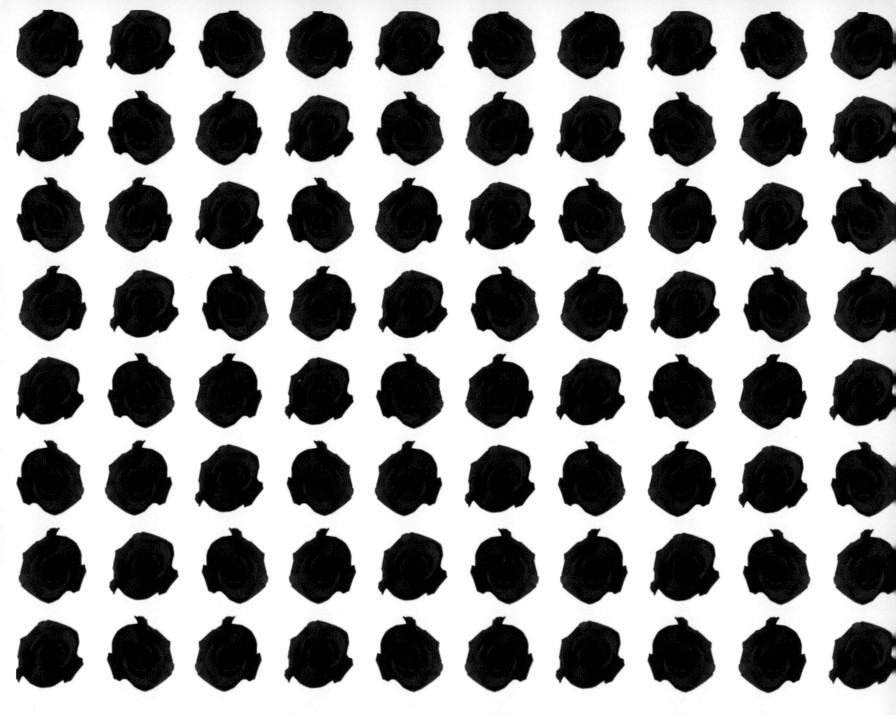

Edgar Allan Poe wrote "The Raven." We named our football team after his poem. For 60 years on his birthday, January 19th, an unknown visitor left 3 roses at his grave.

60 years x 3 roses = how many roses for Poe?

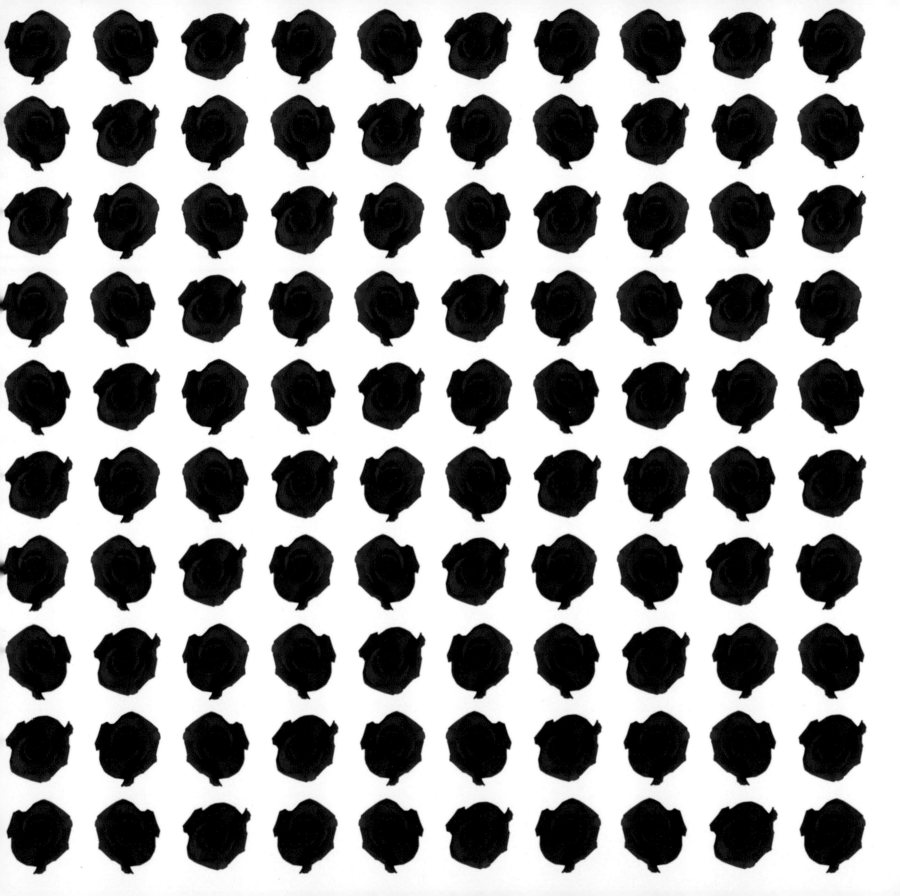

(The LEGG MASON Building
is Baltimore's tallest,
standing 529 feet high)

(The Washington Monument located in the
Mount Vernon neighborhood predates the
well-known monument in Washington DC
by several decades)

84 MT VER

GREAT KIDS
GREAT SCHOOLS

Baltimore is the

20th

(The city is named after Lord Baltimore, converted from "Baile An Ti Mhoir", an Irish term meaning "Town of the Big House")

largest city in
the United States.

(Founded in 1977, Baltimore City Paper is a weekly alternative newspaper providing information on the local theater, concerts and local restaurants)

Maryland's state flower is the Black-eyed Susan.

Can you find **21** of them on another page in this book?

Baltimore teacher James Ryder Randall was 22 years old when he wrote "Maryland, My Maryland."

The despot's heel is on thy shore,
Maryland!
is torch is at thy temple door,
Maryland!
Avenge the patriotic gore,
That flecked the streets of Baltim
Maryland! My Maryland
Maryland.

23 diamondback terrapins- the official mascot of the University of **Maryland.** The terrapin is the **only turtle in** America to live in brackish water.

The largest ever
caught was 9 inches.

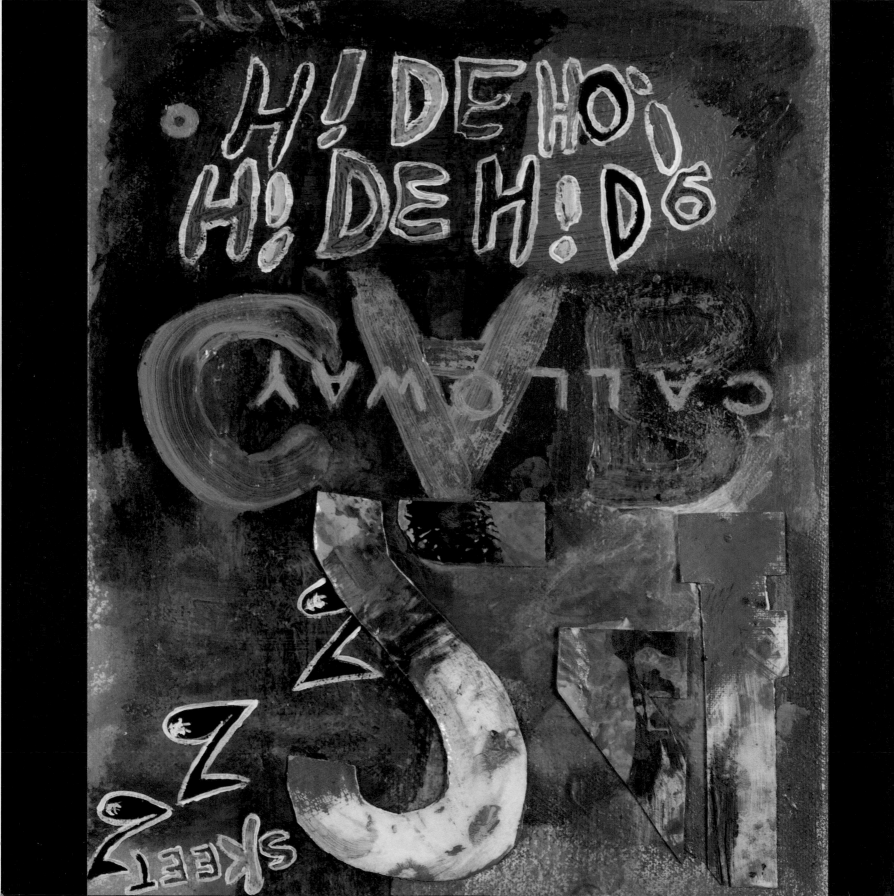

Cab Calloway was **24** when he recorded his hit jazz tune **"Minnie the Moocher."**

Jacob Fussell charged 25¢ for two pints of ice cream. In 1851 he opened the first ice cream business in the USA.

Baltimore Artists

0 – Carbery Morrow

makes ceramic pieces from coils and slabs of earthenware and stoneware clay, and hand-painted glazes. She is drawn to hand-building techniques because of the imperfect and organic forms that emerge. Imperfection best models life, complete with nuance, texture, asymmetry, and the welcome "accidents."

Her work is available at the Farnsworth Museum Store in Rockland, Maine; Unburied Treasure Artisan's Gallery in Surf City, NC; and at her studio in Owings Mills, MD.

www.carberymorrow.com

1 – Marion Stern

became a lifelong student of watercolor the first time she watched a demonstration of the medium over 30 years ago. In each of the many places she has lived, a top priority has been finding a circle of "watercolor friends" and instructors. She earned a BFA from Towson University and is a signature member of the Baltimore Watercolor Society. She strives to produce paintings that exhibit the exciting and unique elements of watercolor that attracted her to the medium – its spontaneity, transparency, sparkling whites and unpredictability. An avid gardener, she finds flowers, with their endless variety, one of her favorite subjects.

marionjstern@aol.com

2 – Tom Chalkley

is a cartoonist and illustrator from Baltimore. He specializes in caricatures and cartoon maps, but as a life-long dinosaur geek, he leapt at the chance to draw a realistic Astrodon.

www.tomchalk.com

3 – Bonnie Matthews

has been drawing critters since age 3! She created a career out of her passion for paint. She has a degree in Communication Arts and Design from Virginia Commonwealth University.

After working as a graphic designer for 8 years, she turned back to her roots and started freelancing as an illustrator. Bonnie's work is very versatile and appeals to both children and adults. She has a prestigious client list including Wellpoint Blue Cross, National Geographic, Smithsonian Institution, and Simon & Schuster. She also paints custom paintings and murals for people and corporations.

www.bonniematthews.com

4 – Jessica Pegorsch

is an artist and educator who recently returned to Baltimore to open Tilt Studio, Inc., a design studio located in Charles Village. At Tilt, Jess is the acting Artist in Residence and her duties include arts representation and community liaison. Jess' interests lie in creating new opportunities and connecting resources for the ever-expanding Baltimore arts scene.

www.jessicampegorsch.com

5 – Amanda Brodsky

is a freelance artist in Baltimore. In addition to illustration and graphic design work, she does such decorative painting as faux finishes and wall murals.

www.amandabrodsky.com

6 – Wayne Arnold

is a cinematographer and independent film maker. He is a student of light and

Baltimore Artists

shadow. His three muses are reflection, refraction, and transmission of light.

cinemafotog@yahoo.com

7 – Kevin O'Malley

is the author and illustrator of over 70 picture books. He has lived in Baltimore for 30 years with his wife and two children.

www.booksbyomalley.com

8 – Taylor Goff

In addition to being a freelance designer, she is an art director at Weber Shandwick, a design and marketing agency. She graduated in 2007 from Stevenson University with a BS in Visual Communications.

Here are a few words and phrases that either fill her day, dreams or heart: Art, conceptual thinking, family, painting, night-time games, friends, simplicity, color, warm springs, warm summers, warm falls and warm winters, secrets, creativity, perfect solutions, holidays, a morning cup of coffee, shelled walnuts and pecans, putting sweat and tears into something you truly love, opportunity, and happy endings.

taylordesign@yahoo.com

9 – Cristian A. Alba

has a BA in sculpture from Towson University and has been doing figurative work out of Baltimore for seven years. He works as an exhibit technician at the Port Discovery Children's Museum and is an assistant teacher for after-school art programs at the Creative Alliance.

cristian.alba@hotmail.com

10 – Michel Modell

was born in San Diego, California. As the youngest child of a military family she became well versed in traveling the world and translating her environment in a creative manner. After graduating with a Bachelor of Science in Ocean Engineering from Florida Tech, Michel returned to her first love of figure skating and joined a variety of traveling shows both domestic and worldwide.

After retiring from professional figure skating in 1998, Michel began to explore other mediums of expression outside the realm of performing arts. This exploration led her to take continuing education classes at both Maryland Institute College of Art (MICA) and the Corcoran College of Art.

Michel completed her Master's in the Hoffberger School of Painting at MICA in May 2010. She currently serves as Vice-President of the Board at Maryland Art Place and other local committees to promote sponsorship of the Arts within the Baltimore community.

www.michelmodell.com

11 – Annie Gray Robrecht

After receiving a BFA from MICA, Annie Gray found that Baltimore was home. She specializes in constant dabbling between the realms of art and craft. Her influences include dinosaurs, primitive cultures, obsessive patterns, and dirt.

www.fringekissedcrafts.blogspot.com

12 – Anne Stiebing

Born into a family of artists and educators, Anne Stiebing was instilled with creativity and compassion as well as the drive to pursue her interests to their fullest. It was through Girl Scouts that she developed a love of the environment and a sense of duty to serve the community. She expresses her passion for art, environmentalism and

Baltimore Artists

community through her work as a fiber artist and through teaching art. Anne earned her BFA and Masters of Arts in Teaching from MICA. She teaches at the Creative Alliance and is a Girl Scout troop leader.

annestiebing@gmail.com

13 – Jennifer Berk

has been painting in acrylic medium for the past 10 years, studying abstract, landscape, and figurative painting under a variety of accomplished, nationally known painters. In her work she attempts to combine vivid color with expressionist gestures to create strong images for the viewer.

Abstract painting is a welcomed departure from life's routines, schedules, and expectations. It presents overwhelming freedoms: no schedule, no plan, no preconceived image, no step-by-step instructions. There is only a blank canvas, a focus on the process, and a flow to a final destination. Landscape painting is also a journey: preserving the color and richness of nature in a lasting image.

jenniferberk.com

14 – Mary Gearhart

worked in Manhattan for 25 years in photography, dance and theater arts. She designed lighting for the stage and photographed performing arts events in NYC and abroad, touring with the Mimi Garrard Dance Co., Sarah Skaggs Dance and the Wooster Group. Her photographs have been published internationally in academic and arts journals, textbooks, The New York Times, Dance Magazine, Village Voice, and Time Out. She founded and ran the Mary Gearhart Gallery on Mott St. in Little Italy in the late 90's, where she curated and exhibited work by over 100 artists. She now lives and works in Baltimore, MD, and Raquette Lake, NY. Her son Coby (age 9) collaborated on collage 14.

15 – Maren Hassinger and Ava Hassinger

Ava Hassinger received her BFA in Photography and Imaging in 2008 at New York University. Hassinger freelances as a photographer, curator, writer, and graphic designer.

Maren Hassinger earned her BA from Bennington College and completed her MFA at UCLA in Los Angeles. She

is the Director of the Rinehart School of Graduate Sculpture at MICA. Her sculpture and peformance have long been concerned with nature, motion, and loss – themes that have more recently expanded to address issues of identity. Hassinger has participated in numerous solo and group exhibitions and performances. Among her many significant awards and achievements, Hassinger received the Adolph and Esther Gottlieb Foundation Grant, the Anonymous Was a Woman Grant, and the Lifetime Achievement Award.

www.marenhassinger.com

16 – Kim Manfredi

was awarded both the Hoffberger and Polovoy Merit scholarships and earned her MFA at the Hoffberger School of Painting in May 2009. She graduated cum laude with a BFA in painting from MICA in 1988. Recent exhibitions include C. Grimaldis Gallery, Sublime Structure, Conner Contemporary Art, Options Biennial Exhibition, and Hemphill Fine Arts. Kim was a semi-finalist for the 2009 Janet and Walter Sondheim prize and participated in the Maryland Art Place Critics' Residency Program curated

Baltimore Artists

by Vincent Katz. Most recently she has been nominated for the 185th Annual: An Invitational Exhibition of Contemporary American Art at the National Academy Museum.

www.kimmanfredi.com

17 – Melody Often

is a crab and comic book creator whose undergrad thesis, In The Hands Of Boys, won the 2005 Xeric Grant. She attended MICA for Illustration and Literature and resides in a warehouse in the Station North Arts District.

www.melodyoften.blogspot.com

18 – Steve Baker

With an undeniable sense of warmth, space and creativity, Steve Baker harnesses his passion into everything from fences of recycled oil drums to sinks out of recycled windowpanes. His earthen, organically whimsical pieces encompass Whollyterra's complex simplicity. Steve is able to capture beauty and bring it to another dimension of reality. He takes existing elements and remakes them into art durable enough to last the life times that he hopes to make better

with his pieces.

www.whollyterra.com

19 – Mina Cheon

(Korean-American), PhD, MFA, is a new media artist, writer, and educator who divides her time between Baltimore, New York, and Seoul, Korea. She is currently a full-time professor at MICA, teaching studio, new media, and liberal arts. Recently, her book SHAMANISM + CYBERSPACE (2009, Atropos Press, New York and Dresden) has been published and shared widely. As an artist, she has shown internationally, with solo exhibitions at spaces including the Lance Fung Gallery in New York (2002); Insa Art Space, Arts Council, Seoul (2005); and C. Grimaldis Gallery in Baltimore (2008).

Cheon chose the number 19 and the story of Edgar Allan Poe for the conceptual possibilities of playing with multiplication as a part of counting numbers. While seeing an array of roses, a child can count all 180 of them, do a multiplication of the rows, or read the text for a different kind of multiplication process. As an artistic process, Cheon worked with a real

rose, photographed it, and then digitally manipulated the single rose in various angles so that the roses seem to be moving and in action. Also, for the artist, it was especially nice to know that Poe received so many roses over the years and to be able to lay out that number for readers to see at a single glance.

www.minacheon.com

20 – Kenny Yee

is a Baltimore painter and teaching artist with strong ties to Long Island and Queens, New York. Kenny finds enjoyment in working with kids, drinking coffee, and walking around aimlessly (he never combines the three). He's thankful for this opportunity and acknowledges that the endless support from his wife and family makes everything possible.

www.kennethyee.com

21 – Siiri Poldmae

was born and raised in Baltimore and attended the University of the Arts in Philadelphia, where she received her BFA in printmaking. She has two very entertaining and wonderful children

Baltimore Artists

and one wonderful husband (also entertaining, for the record). She imagines the eggs in her piece have a diverse diet which includes all kinds of plant life, rocks and dirt (nature in general), and fruit. They love sweets and butter and especially chocolate, as well as odd stuff like glue and plastic. They are generally pleasant and helpful, though prone to misfortune.

siiripmcc@gmail.com

22 – Gregg Simonton

is a self-taught painter from Georgia. He has exhibited up and down the east coast since the mid 90's. In addition to painting he produces television commercials and writes about music. He lives in the Patterson Park neighborhood of Baltimore with his wife Sharon, daughter Sofia, and dog Inka. He would like to thank Marsha Derrickson for getting him involved in this project, and, of course, Siri Lise Doub for all her help and patience. His contribution is dedicated to his father.

www.greggsimonton.com

23 – Michelle La Perriere

Before moving to Maryland, Michelle La Perriere thought that duckpins could fly, and that terrapins were used in bowling. Born and raised in Denver, Colorado, she knew she was an artist when she was four. Michelle came to Baltimore many moons ago to study at MICA, where she currently teaches and has done lots of administrative work. Michelle loves to draw (on nearly everything), to paint, make short films, write poetry, and act theatrically. She also loves to travel, speak fake foreign languages with her daughter, and to stand on her head. She believes in being kind (although sometimes has to work really hard at it), and that we all need to cherish the earth, turtles, ducks and all.

www.michellelaperriere.com

24 – Jeffrey Kent

has a commitment to communicating ideas through creative expression and a dedication to community service from ideals he learned as a youth. He learned the importance of sharing his time and knowledge with our youths, teaching them to set goals and to recognize the possibilities within their grasp. In 2003 Kent founded Baltimore's Sub-Basement Artist Studios, an underground, artist-run studio and gallery. Kent is currently a 2010 Masters in Fine Art candidate in the Hoffberger School of Painting at MICA. The artistic vision of Kent is an important contribution to the continuous spectrum of urban cultural expression and identity.

www.jeffreykentart.com

25 – Melissa Dickenson

received her Bachelors of Fine Art from MICA in 2002. She has exhibited her work locally in Maryland at the Baltimore Museum of Art, the Rosenberg Gallery at Goucher College, Gallery Imperato, and nationally at Rodger Lapelle Galleries in Philadelphia, Anno Dommini and Thinkspace Galleries, both in California, as well as Transformer Gallery and American University in Washington, D.C. Internationally, Melissa has shown her work at Youkobo Art Space in Tokyo, Japan. Dickenson is a recipient of Maryland State Artist Awards in both 2006 and 2008, as well as a finalist for

Baltimore Artists

the Walter and Janet Sondheim Prize for 2008 and semi-finalist for both the Bethesda Painting Award and the Trawick Prize in 2009. Most recently she was awarded an Artist Grant to attend Masia Can Serrat, Barcelona, Spain, for fellowship in 2009.

Dickenson's work is also part of the permanent collection of the Embassy of Sudan.

www.melissadickenson.com

Cover – James R. Long

received his BFA in sculpture from Indiana University of Pennsylvania in 1994, his MFA in sculpture from Bowling Green State University in 1996, and his MA in art education from Teachers College, Columbia University, in 2003. Long was a recipient of two fellowships, a Peace Corps Fellowship and an American India Foundation Fellowship, for his work in art education. He has exhibited his work at many venues including the Austin Museum of Art in Texas, Ghana's National Museum, Columbia University in New York City, and many galleries in Baltimore. He was an art teacher at Frederick Douglass High School in Baltimore for three years and a sculpting instructor in MICA's continuing education program. Long's work explores the use of simple utilitarian forms that when together convey a greater meaning. His paintings examine the creation of graphic language as expressed through the art work of children. While working in the New York Public Schools and in India with street children, Long became fascinated by a child's development of schema. As a means to understand this process, he began appropriating his student's images.

www.jamesrlong.com